Micro Business for Teens
Workbook

Carol Topp, CPA

Published by Ambassador Publishing
Cincinnati, Ohio

ISBN 978-0-9829245-2-5

Cover Design: Dave Huff
Author Photo: Cathy Lyons

Disclaimer and Limitation of Liability
This book is designed to provide accurate and authoritative information about the subject matter covered. The author is not rending legal, accounting, or other professional advice.

The fact that a company, organization or website is mentioned does not mean that the author endorses the information or services provided. The resources mentioned in this book should be evaluated by the reader. Readers should also be aware that organizations and web sites mentioned may have been changed or ceased operations since the publication of this book.

Any tax advice contained in this book was not intended or written to be used, and cannot be used, by any taxpayer for the purpose of avoiding penalties that may be imposed under the Internal Revenue Code or applicable state or local tax law provisions. Furthermore, this book was not intended or written to support the promotion or marketing of any of the transactions or matters it may address.

Table of Contents

How to Use This Book   5

Chapter One: What is a Micro Business?   7

Chapter Two: Getting an Idea   15

Chapter Three: Problems and Pitfalls   21

Chapter Four: Writing a Business Plan   27

Chapter Five: Starting Without Debt or Risk   41

Chapter Six: Research and Learning More   45

Chapter Seven: Encouragement   49

Chapter Eight: Sales   53

Chapter Nine: Marketing   59

Chapter Ten: Customer Service   71

Chapter Eleven: Record Keeping   73

Chapter Twelve: Bookkeeping & Software   77

Chapter Thirteen: Names, Numbers and Insurance   87

Chapter Fourteen: Time Management   93

Conclusion   99

About the Author   101

How To Use This Book

Individual use

This workbook is designed to be used in conjunction with the Micro Business for Teens books, *Starting a Micro Business* and *Running a Micro Business*. You may order these books at **MicroBusinessForTeens.com**. Read the corresponding chapter in *Starting a Micro Business* or *Running a Micro Business* first, then complete the workbook pages. Work at your own pace. It may take you only a few days or several weeks depending on your time and effort. If you complete a chapter a week, you can complete the entire workbook in about 3 months.

I highly recommend finding a mentor to advise you as you work through this workbook. An advisor may be your parents or a small business owner. Discuss your workbook answers, especially your business plan, with your mentor. They can provide accountability and useful feedback.

Consider enrolling in the *Micro Business for Teens* virtual class, an on-line class where you can interact with the instructor and other teenagers starting their micro business. Visit **MicroBusinessforTeens.com** for more information.

Classroom or group use

This workbook can be easily adapted for group use. A realistic schedule would be to cover one chapter a week, taking 14 weeks for the full course. Some groups may progress faster. Alternatively, the curriculum can be expanded by inviting guest speakers, or spreading out some chapters, particularly the creation of a business plan, over several weeks.

I recommend that students read the corresponding chapter in *Starting a Micro Business* or *Running a Micro Business* and complete the workbook pages before class. Use class time to discuss the chapter, and to share results and ideas with others.

The classroom teacher can serve as a mentor, or outside mentors, such as small business owners, can be invited to assist the students, especially in reviewing business plans.

Some groups find it helpful to organize a trade fair as a capstone project. Each student displays his or her business idea complete with business cards and a sales presentation at the trade fair. Friends, family and community members can be invited to learn about the students' businesses. The trade fair serves as an incentive to complete the workbook as the class progresses.

Students should consider enrolling in the Micro Business for Teens virtual class where they can interact with the on-line instructor and other teenagers starting their micro businesses. The virtual class can compliment the live classroom as students post answers to the workbook questions in a common, shared website. It can motivate a student to complete the homework such as their marketing plan, and post it to the virtual class website for others to see. Visit **MicroBusinessforTeens.com** for more information.

The *Micro Business for Teens Workbook* is very flexible and can be used as best fits the needs of your group. Feel free to share comments on your experiences at **Micro-BusinessforTeens.com**.

Chapter One
What is a Micro Business?

In the book *Starting a Micro Business*, Chapter One lists 8 characteristics of a micro business:

- Simple and _profitable_
- Only one worker _The owner_
- Sole proprietorship which means _only one owner_
- Little start up money needed or completely _debt free_
- Usually _homebased_
- Low risk
- _manageable_
- Learn while _earning_

Which appeals to you most? _Only one worker_

Why? _I can work alone_

Discuss in your group or with a mentor or parent what you desire most in a micro business.

What concerns do you have?

Define Entrepreneur

Using page 21 in *Starting a Micro Business* or a dictionary define "entrepreneur":

Is it necessary to be an "entrepreneur" to start a micro business? Why (or why not)?

Do you have what it takes?

It's helpful to have certain personality traits to succeed in starting a micro business. No one has all these traits, but I bet you're good at something!

	I need help with this	Some-where in between	One of my strengths
Creativity		✓	
Initiative		✓	
Courage	✓		
Organization			✓
Drive/Ambition		✓	
Perseverance		✓	
Vision	✓		
Problem solving		✓	
Hard working		✓	
Honesty			✓
Self-discipline	✓		
Responsibility			✓
Goal oriented			✓

If you lack any of these traits, are you doomed to failure? Certainly not! Starting a micro business will let you practice to improve your weaknesses. You'll learn a lot about business-and yourself– as you make money!

Get Ready for Chapter Two: Getting An Idea

In Chapter Two you will start considering an idea for a micro business that you could start. Where do good ideas come from? They may come from your own experiences, skills and talents. They may spring from brainstorming other ideas or they can come from seeing a need.

Meeting a Need

For the next few days, notice every time someone complains or gets frustrated with a product. Think of creative ways to meet a need that you see.

Example: During the spring, our neighbors garbage cans roll down the street on windy days. They need someone to collect the cans and return them to their places. That's an idea for a micro business!

I heard complaints about...

I see a need for...

Listing your experiences and skills can prompt some business ideas..

My skills and abilities. Example: create a blog, change a diaper, bathe a dog, etc...

My jobs: babysitting, mowing grass, etc.

List your talents and hobbies. They are great building blocks for a micro business.

My talents. Examples: piano, paint watercolors, sing, act, etc...

My hobbies such as playing guitar, scrapbooking, photography, etc.

Brainstorming

Before going on and picking a business idea, it is helpful to brainstorm a bit. Keep an open mind, listing everything that comes into your head, even if you can already think of problems with the idea. Now is not the time to evaluate your ideas; that comes later.

Brainstorming in a group is also fun as ideas spark other ideas. Be considerate of everyone's ideas. What may sound unrealistic to you, could be a the perfect micro business for someone else.

Rules for brainstorming ideas:
(from http://www.brainstorming.co.uk/tutorials/brainstormingrules.html)

Rule 1: Postpone and withhold your judgment of ideas
Do not pass judgment on ideas until the completion of the brainstorming session. Do not suggest that an idea won't work or that it has negative side-effects. All ideas are potentially good so don't judge them until afterwards. At this stage, avoid discussing the ideas at all, as this will inevitably involve either criticizing or complimenting them. The evaluation of ideas takes up valuable brain power which should be devoted to the creation of ideas. Maximize your brainstorming session by only spending time generating new ideas.

Rule 2: Encourage wild and exaggerated ideas
It's much easier to tame a wild idea than it is to think of an immediately valid one in the first place. The 'wilder' the idea the better. Shout out bizarre and unworkable ideas to see what they spark off. No idea is too ridiculous. State any outlandish ideas. Exaggerate ideas to the extreme.

Rule 3: Quantity counts at this stage, not quality
Go for quantity of ideas at this point; narrow down the list later. The more creative ideas a person or a group has to choose from, the better. If the number of ideas at the end of the session is very large, there is a greater chance of finding a really good idea. Keep each idea short, do not describe it in detail - just capture its essence. Brief clarifications can be requested. Think fast, reflect later.

Rule 4: Build on the ideas put forward by others
Build and expand on the ideas of others. Try and add extra thoughts to each idea. Use other people's ideas as inspiration for your own. Combine several of the suggested ideas to explore new possibilities. It's just as valuable to be able to adapt and improve other people's ideas as it is to generate the initial idea that sets off new trains of thought.

Brainstorm some micro business. Start with a word in a bubble. Branch out with other words related to the starting word and go from there. Here's an example:

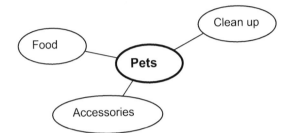

Now you practice adding to the Pets brainstorm or come up with your own starter word.

Be creative and even wild!

Here are some possible starter words to get your ideas flowing:

Fashion   Cars   Music   Food   Games   Health   Horses

Try and fill up the page.

Chapter Two
Getting an Idea

Hopefully your brainstorming from Chapter One has resulted in a list of talents, skills and interest you have. In a group, or by yourself, you should have come up with some possible micro business ideas.

Read Chapter Two of *Starting a Micro Business*. Add to your brainstorming list anything new that comes to mind from that chapter. It is okay to copy another great idea!

Pick at least three and up to five of the ideas that appeal to you most:

1. Custom couches
2. Custom firearms
3. motorized couches
4. _____
5. _____

Next you will create a mini business plan for each idea. This is not a full business plan (you'll do that in Chapter Four). This is called an elevator speech. Try and tell someone your idea in the time it takes to ride an elevator, about one to two minutes.

For each of your 3 to 5 best micro business ideas, explain your product or service, why it is needed, who will buy it and why they will buy from you.

Example: My micro business idea is to photograph senior pictures (*a service*). Every senior in my youth group (*the customer*) wants some nice pictures taken outdoors, but many cannot afford a professional (*the need*). I will charge less than half what a professional does, I'm good at photography and as a bonus I can make a scrapbook album for my customer (*why you*).

3rd: motorized couches
we would put a huge engine and attach it to your couch

9st: custom couches
- custom couch design.
- custom fabrics
- custom decal
Custom everything

2nd: custom firearms
- custom stocks
- custom upgrades
- custom everything really

For each of your 3 to 5 best micro business ideas, explain your product or service, why it is needed, who will buy it and why they will buy from you.

The next step is to do a small market survey and ask your mentor or teacher, parents and friends about your idea. Give them your elevator speech sales pitch and ask for their opinion. Record their reactions and any advice they offer:

	My mentor/teacher	My parents	My friends	Other/classmates
Idea #1 custom couches				
Idea #2 custom firearms				
Idea #3 motorized couches				
Idea #4				
Idea #5				

Wrap Up Chapter Two Getting An Idea.

So far, you have used several techniques to come up with an idea:

- Brainstorming
- Listing your skills, talents and hobbies
- Reading others' ideas from *Starting a Micro Business*
- Narrowing your list and creating an elevator speech
- Asking for the opinions of others you know

Now, you need to narrow the list to only one idea (or at most two ideas, if you are feeling ambitious). Select one micro business to focus on at this time:

_____

Congratulations! You've actually accomplished quite a bit. Some teenagers never brainstorm ideas or see themselves as micro business owners. You can be different. You are unique and your idea is unique in some special way.

We will investigate your idea in more detail in the next few chapters, so get ready for some work that will be very worthwhile and help you to be successful.

*Why not share your idea with other students? Drop a comment at the **MicroBusinessForTeens.com** website or Facebook page. If it's a really fantastic idea that you don't want anyone to steal, just be a little vague with the details.*

Chapter Three
Problems and Pitfalls

Problems with Products

In Chapter Three of *Starting a Micro Business*, there is a listing of the problems with selling products. List the 10 problems below:

_____   _____

_____   _____

_____   _____

_____   _____

_____   _____

Which of these problems might apply to your micro business?

❏ None
❏ Some, especially _____
❏ Almost all of them!

Consider which of the solutions offered might work for you:

❏ Sell digital products
❏ Drop shipping
❏ Order after sale is complete
❏ Shipping service

❏ Order one month in advance
❏ Give away low cost items
❏ Discontinue some items
❏ Other:_____

Make a plan to implement a solution. List the steps you may need to take, what you may need to learn, what topics to research, and who to ask for advice.

Plan to Avoid Problems and Pitfalls With Products:

My chosen solution: _____

Steps I need to take:

What I need to learn:

Topics I need to research:

People I can ask for advice:

Problems with Services

Some micro businesses focus on providing services instead of products. Service-oriented may also have problems and pitfalls. List the problems mentioned in Chapter Three of *Starting a Micro Business*.

_____   _____

Which of these problems might apply to your micro business?

❏ None

❏ One, especially _____

❏ Both of them!

Consider which of the solutions offered might work for you:

❏ Hire help   ❏ Increase your price

❏ Pass it along   ❏ Learn customer service skills

❏ Sell your knowledge   ❏ Listen to customers' wants

Make a plan to implement a solution. List the steps you may need to take, what you may need to learn, what topics to research, and who to ask for advice.

Plan to Avoid Problems and Pitfalls With Services:

My chosen solution: _____

Steps I need to take:

What I need to learn:

Topics I need to research:

People I can ask for advice:

The Problems with Partners

I discourage partnerships for teenager micro business owners. List the problems mentioned in Chapter Three of *Starting a Micro Business*.

_____   _____

_____   _____

Which of these problems might apply to your micro business?

❏ None

❏ One, especially _____

❏ All of them!

Make a plan to implement a solution. List the steps you may need to take, what you may need to learn, what topics to research, and who to ask for advice.

Plan to Avoid Problems and Pitfalls With Partners

My chosen solution: _____

Steps I need to take:

What I need to learn:

Topics I need to research:

People I can ask for advice:

Chapter Four
Writing a Business Plan

In this chapter you will write up a business plan. A business plan is a way for you to think and plan on paper before you start your business. A plan can help you avoid a lot of mistakes, prevent you from wasting time and save you money.

In Chapter Four of *Starting a Micro Business*, I list the three parts of a business plan and what is covered in each part:

1. _____ covers

_____

2. _____ covers

_____

3. _____ covers

_____

Business Plan

for

_____

(name of your micro business)

Business Concept

Product or Service:_____

Describe your product or service:

What makes your product or service unique?

Describe the industry (i.e pet food, clothing, education, auto repair, retail, food, etc.) and explain the need for your product or service:

What are the new trends in your industry?

Is there opportunity for you in your industry?

How will you measure success? Will it be a financial goal or based on sales/number of customers?

Define your goal in numbers ($, people or sales units):

Example: I want to make enough profit to finance a ski trip in January. Total cost will be $400.

What do you hope to learn by starting this micro business?

What knowledge, experience and skills do you possess that will be helpful in your business?

What knowledge do you lack?

You may need some professionals to guide you:

List an accountant who can help you:

Name:_____   Phone:_____

List a lawyer who can help you:

Name:_____   Phone:_____

List an insurance agent who can help you:

Name:_____   Phone:_____

List an experienced business owner who can help you:

Name:_____   Phone:_____

What licenses and permits are required to operate your business?

Examples include EIN (Employer Identification Number from the IRS), vendor's license, sales tax permit, assumed name registration, zoning permit, food preparation permit.

Marketing Plan

Customers

Who are your potential customers?

How will you reach potential customers? Where will you find them?

How much will you spend (in time and money) doing marketing? Be as specific as possible and include website costs.

Competition

Who is your competition?

What are your competitors' strengths?

What are your competitors' weaknesses?

How will you stand out? Why will people buy from you and not your competition?

Surveys

Tell at least five people about your product or service. Ask them: Would you buy from me? How much would you pay?

Record what they said:

Name	Would you buy from me?	What price would you pay?

Risks

What are your major areas of risk? What can break? What can go wrong? What money could you lose?

Financial Plan

Start Up Expenses

Equipment

What start up equipment is needed? Will you need a computer, a desk, an oven?

Where will it come from? Does your family already own the equipment? Ask your parents' permission to use it.

Will you need to buy some equipment? What will it cost to purchase?

Equipment Needed	Parental Approval	Own or Need to Buy?	Cost to Buy

Storage

What storage or preparation space is needed? Where will it come from? Does your family have the space? Ask your parents' permission to use it! Will you need to rent space? What will it cost to rent?

Space Needed	Parental Approval	Own or Need to Rent?	Cost to Rent Space

Other Start Up Expenses

What other startup expenses will you have? Get specific costs.

Item	Cost
Advertising	
Professional advice	
Licenses and permits	
Starting inventory	
Supplies	
Other:	
Total Start Up Expenses	

Initial Funding for Start Up Expenses

Where will your initial funding come from? *Examples: your savings, a job, mom and dad, gifts, investors.*

Source of Start Up Funds	Amount

If you are borrowing money from family or friends, what is the repayment plan? Be specific with dates or milestones and amounts.

Lender	Amount Owed	Payment	Frequency	Pay Off Date

Item Cost

Fixed Costs: List costs that do not vary with the amount of sales. These are spent regardless of how many sales you make. *Examples are your monthly internet charge, loan repayment, cell phone use, rental space, professional advice, advertising, website.*

Fixed Costs	Amount each month (or year)
Total Fixed Cost	per month (or per year)

Variable Costs (or Cost of Goods Sold): List costs that vary with the amount of sales. *Examples: material to produce your product, merchant fees per sale, shipping and packaging costs. Do not include your own labor; it comes out of your profit. Variable Costs are also called Cost of Goods Sold.*

Variable Costs	Amount per unit sold
Total Variable Cost per Unit	per unit

(Repeat as necessary for each unique product)

Profit

What profit do you hope to make on each item sold or customer serviced? *If you are unsure start by adding 25-50% of the cost to be your profit.*

Pricing

What will you charge?

If you are unsure try this equation: 1.25 * Variable Cost per Unit = $_____ / unit (that would be 25% markup on your variable costs)

Is it reasonable?

What do your competitors charge?

Sales

What are your estimated sales for the first three months, the next three months and the first year? *You can start with number of products sold or number of customers serviced, but then calculate the dollars of sales.*

	Sales (in units or customers)	Sales in dollars
First 3 months' sales		
3-6 months' sales		
Sales for first year		

Break Even Analysis

Add all the Fixed Costs (from pages 32 and 33)

Start Up Expenses $_____

Fixed Costs $_____

Total Fixed Costs for first year: $_____

Total Variable Costs (from page 33): $_____

Margin per unit = Selling Price per Unit – Variable Cost per Unit

This is a measure of how much profit you make for each unit sold.

= $_____ – $ _____

= $_____ per unit

Break even point = Total Fixed Costs / Margin per Unit

This is how many units you must sell in the first year to break even.

= $_____ / $_____ per unit

= _____ units

Is it reasonable? Can you sell that much?

Collect data

Fill in the gray areas in the chart below with the numbers from your business plan.

Calculate the other lines as indicated.

		Product #1	Product #2	Product #3	Total
1	Number sold in one year				
2	Selling Price per unit				
3	Variable Cost per unit				
4	Fixed Costs				
5	Margin per unit (Line 2 - Line 3)				
6	Break Even Point in units (Line 4/Line 5)				
7	Total Sales (Line 1 * Line 2)				
8	Total COGS(Line 1 * Line 3)				
9	Gross Profit (Line 7 – Line 8)				

Projected Income Statement for First Year

Income

        Total Sales (from the chart above, Total column) $

        Other Income (interest on savings, etc) $\underline{\hspace{3cm}}$.

Total Income $

Less Cost of Goods Sold (COGS from the chart)   ($\underline{\hspace{3cm}}$)

Gross Profit (Income – COGS, from the chart above) $

Expenses (list separately)

        Start Up Costs $

        Advertising $

        Professional advice $

        Supplies $

        Other $

Total Expenses $\underline{\hspace{3cm}}$.

Net Income (Gross Profit- Expenses) $

Chapter Five
Starting Without Debt or Risk

To start a micro business you may need equipment, inventory, advertising or other expenses. While creating your business plan in Chapter Four of this workbook, you should have considered all your start up expenses. Summarize all your start up expenses:

Expense	Amount
Equipment	$ 6,000
Space	$ fin land sized warehouse
Advertising	$ cons
Professional Advice	$
Licenses and permits	$
Inventory	$
Supplies	$ wood, engines
Other	$
Total Start Up expenses	$

What's Wrong With Debt?

In Chapter Five of *Starting a Micro Business*, I list several reasons why debt should be avoided. Fill in the blanks using *Starting a Micro Business*.

Debt presumes _____ .

The use of debt or borrowing encourages _____ .

Being in debt makes you _____ **to the lender.**

Taking on debt _____ **your risk of failure.**

Explain why:

Debt can stop _____

Answers: upon the future, quick or rash decisions; a slave; increases, unable to use profit to grow business; blessings.

42

MicroBusinessForTeens.com

Where Will The Money Come From?

Chapter Five of *Starting a Micro Business*, lists several ways to fund your micro business start up. Check which ideas will work for you and estimate the amounts as best you can.

- Savings can provide: $_____

- I plan to ask _____

     For a loan of $_____

     Or to be my investor with $_____

- Selling some stuff will bring in cash:

Item_____   Amount I could get for it: $_____

Item_____   Amount I could get for it: $_____

Item_____   Amount I could get for it: $_____

- Work a temporary job to raise some cash at:

Place/Job:_____   Amount I could make: $_____

Place/Job:_____   Amount I could make: $_____

Place/Job:_____   Amount I could make: $_____

Total of all sources of Start Up money: $_____

How close are you to the total start up expenses listed on the previous page?

Still short? Rework your plan. See if you can cut some start up expenses or increase your start up money.

Chapter Six
Research and Learning More

Read Chapter Six Taking Care of Business from *Starting a Micro Business*.

Continue to research more about your chosen micro business idea by using at least one book, one website and one person. *Starting a Micro Business* has several recommendations of books and websites to get you started. Record your research on the following pages:

One helpful book was _____
(title) by _____ (author)
 Things I learned:

One helpful book or website was _____

Things I learned:

Another book or website was _____

Things I learned:

One helpful website was _____

Things I learned:

Another website was _____

Things I learned:

Chapter Seven
Encouragement

Read Chapter Seven in *Starting a Micro Business* where I offer encouragement.

Starting a micro business can be a lot of hard work. It can also challenge and stretch you, so you must try to keep a positive attitude.

Entrepreneurs Can Change the World

Go to the **MicroBusinessForTeens.com** website and enter "change the world" into the search box. You'll find an inspiring video to watch. Or its on YouTube at **http://www.youtube.com/watch?v=T6MhAwQ64c0**

Share your thoughts about it:

The video on entrepreneurship was:

Real Stories

My blog has some stories of teenagers who run micro businesses at **MicroBusiness-ForTeens.com.**

Read at least three stories. Share how they encouraged you:

Blog post on:_____ encouraged me to/by...

Blog post on: _____encouraged me to/by...

Blog post on: _____encouraged me to/by...

Role Models

One of the best ways to stay encouraged is to have a role model. Find a person who has run a business similar to yours. It does not have to be an exact match, but get as close as possible. Explain you are in a business class and want to ask a few questions. Here are some questions to ask them:

- How did you get started in your business?
- What mistakes did you make?
- Who are your competitors?
- How are you different?
- How do you find your customers?
- How do you set your price?
- What advice do you have for someone wanting to do what you do?

Where can you find a business person to interview? Here are a few places:

- Your neighbors, parents, grandparents, friends and friend's parents.
- Your homeschool network or school business teachers.
- The internet. Email a website owner of a business you respect.

One helpful person I talked to was _____
Things I learned:

Another helpful person I talked to was _____

Things I learned:

Another helpful person I talked to was _____

Things I learned:

Chapter Eight
Sales

Your Tag Line

A tag line should be 5-8 words that describe your product or service and emphasize its greatest benefit. What are your product or services greatest benefits?

Here are some examples of tag lines:

Helping children love to read
Beautiful, handmade dresses

Your source for information on horses
Dance lessons in your home

Practice writing a few different tag lines:

Your Sales Presentation

Include these elements in your sales presentation:
1. Introduce yourself and your business name
2. Brief description of your main product or service
3. Two or three of the main benefits of the product or service
4. A brief demonstration, sample or picture if possible
5. Your tag line
6. Your price
7. How to reach you or order
8. A call to action

Practice writing a few different sales presentations. Try to include each of the 8 elements listed above.

Sales Presentations

Try to include all 8 elements!

Using Your Sales Presentation

Where will you use your sales presentation?

☐ Fliers

☐ Email

☐ Website

☐ Face to face

☐ Trade show, craft show, etc.

☐ Phone calls

☐ Other:_____

Making the Sale

Asking questions can help close a sale. Using the examples in *Running a Micro Business,* write some questions you could use in your business to encourage a customer to buy from you.

When...

Would you...

What...

How...

Can I ...

Order Form

Practice filling in an order form for a customer wanting to purchase something from you. Modify this form to meet your needs.

Order Form		
Company Owner Name: _____		
Phone _____	Website or	_____
Customer Address _____		
Phone _____	Email	_____
Product or Service	**Quantity**	**Price**
Notes or special instructions	**Sub Total**	
	Sales Tax	
	Total	
Price List Item 1: Item 2: Item 3:	Price Price Price	

Invoice or Statement

An invoice or statement is a good tool to remind customers to pay you. Practice filling in an invoice for a customer that owes you money. Modify this form to meet your needs.

Invoice or Statement

Customer
Address
Phone   Email

Date	Product or Service	Total
	Subtotal	
	Late fees	
	Paid	
	Balance Due	

Please remit payment to:
Company

Owner Name:

Address:

Thank you for your business!

Chapter Nine
Marketing

In the chapter on marketing in *Running a Micro Business*, you learned how to create a profile on your customer. Answer the following questions about your customer. Your business may have several types of customers, so fill out a profile for each.

Describe a typical customer.

What is their age?

Where do they go? List physical places and on-line sites

What do they read? Books, magazines, websites

What websites do they visit?

What do they do with their free time?

Where do they spend their money?

Describe a typical customer

What is their age?

Where do they go?

What do they read?

What websites do they visit?

What do they do with their free time?

Where do they spend their money?

Describe a typical customer

What is their age?

Where do they go?

What do they read?

What websites do they visit?

What do they do with their free time?

Where do they spend their money?

Reaching a Local Market

Your customers may be local and your marketing plan might involve passing out fliers and business cards. Create a marketing plan by checking off the methods you will plan to use.

❑ Fliers

❑ Brochures

❑ Postcards

❑ Business cards

❑ Email. Start a list with at least 10 names:_____

_____

_____

❑ Local social networking sites. _____

❑ Articles in local newspapers. Newspaper name:_____

Possible topics (start with at least three):_____

_____

❑ Press releases to local papers. Name:_____

Possible topics (start with at least three):_____

_____

❑ Word of mouth.

❑ Trade shows, flea markets. Names:_____

❑ Other

Designing a Business Card

If you have a local business, a business card can be a great tool to tell others about your business.

The minimum information on a business card includes:

- Your name and business name
- Your title or what you do in the business (i.e. web designer, piano teacher, etc)
- Several ways to contact you. Your email, website, phone number, address, etc.

Here are some tips for designing a business card:

- Your business card must communicate more than just your contact information. Make sure that your card includes a tag line that explains what you do.
- Keep the card simple. Do not use too many fonts. Two is usually enough. Do not crowd in too much information.
- Make your main message (your tag line) clear and easy to find.
- Make your business card easy to read. Use contrasting colors between the background and the type. Light background with dark type works best.
- Your name should be the largest piece of information on your card. Usually your name is centered in the middle or top of the card.
- Use a large enough font to be easily readable.
- Run your business card through a spell checker and double-check your contact information.
- Keep all the information on your business card current. If you change your address or phone number, don't scratch out the old number and write in the new one by hand; get new business cards.
- Horizontal layouts are the most common.

Where to buy business cards

One place to design and print business cards is **Vistaprint.com**. You can design your own card and upload it, or use one of their backgrounds and add your information. Vistaprint's prices are very reasonable. You can even get *free* business cards, but they will have Vistaprint's name on the back and you will be limited on your choice of designs.

Use the space below to design several business cards. Show them to friends, a mentor and potential customers. Ask for suggestions.

Business cards are typically 2" by 3.5", so you may have to write small!

Design a Flier

Tips for eye catching fliers:

- Use your tag line in bold letters near the top
- Include 2-3 major benefits
- Use a picture, photo or cartoon
- Keep the words to a minimum and the design simple
- Add your name and contact information

Reaching a Distant Market

Your customers may be far away and your marketing plan might involve creating a website and using social media. Check off the methods you will plan to use.

❑ Website. Possible names: _____

_____

❑ Blog. Possible names:_____

_____

❑ Articles. Possible topics (start with at least 3):_____

_____

_____

❑ Email list

❑ Newsletters/Ezines

❑ Social networking sites, specifically:_____

_____

❑ Affiliate programs from products I like:_____

_____

❑ Podcasts. Possible topics (start with at least 3):_____

_____

_____

❑ Video/Vlogging. Possible topics (start with at least 3):_____

_____

_____

Create a Website and Blog

To reach your on-line market, it is vital for you to have a website. A blog-based website is best, because you can update your information very easily and quickly yourself. Blogs are also good for ranking high in search engines like Google, because they are updated more often than the old-fashioned website.

With a blog-based website, there is no need to pay a web designer to set up or change your site.

What's a blog?

A blog is a web log. They started as web-based journals or diaries. Now they are popular for sharing all kinds of information including telling customers about your business. My website, **MicroBusinessForTeens.com** is a blog-based website. It has blog entries where I share tips on running a micro business and true stories. It also has static website pages where I share information about who I am and what I sell.

I recommend you try **Wordpress.com** to set up your blog-based website. It is free and easy to learn.

Your Website Name

When you sign up for a free website with Wordpress, you can pick a name for your website, but it will be like this:

   Your_chosen_name.wordpress.com

If you don't like the name Wordpress in your website name, you will have to set up and pay for separate website hosting and a domain name registration.

There are lots of web hosting services out there. I use one called MomWebs.com. (but you don't have to be a mom to use them). They can help you install a Wordpress blog onto your website.

Wordpress Tutorials

Wordpress.com has some excellent tutorials on how to set up an account, add posts (your short entries that can be used to write about your business topic) and add static web pages (pages to your website with content that does not change, such as a page about you or a page describing your products).

Sign up video
wordpress.tv/2009/01/05/signing-up-with-wordpresscom/

Dashboard (the controls of the website)
wordpress.tv/2009/01/05/the-wordpresscom-dashboard-introduction/

Put out a quick post
wordpress.tv/2009/01/05/getting-a-post-out-quickly-with-quickpress/

Add a static page
wordpress.tv/2009/01/14/adding-an-about-me-or-any-other-static-page/

There's a ton to learn, so don't feel overwhelmed. You can add additional features to your blog as your business grows.

Perhaps your could tackle learning Wordpress with a group of friends and share what you each learn.

For now just get a basic website up and start blogging so customers can find you and your micro business!

Content for Your Website

Before you create a website, you need to plan what you will say. Write up what you want to have on your home page. Include a greeting, your tag line and what static pages your website will have.

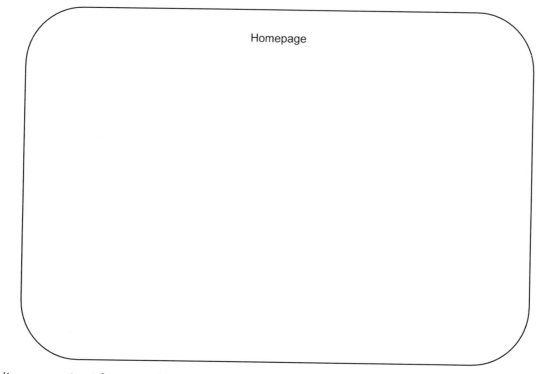

Homepage

Write up content for your About page. Describe yourself and why you started your business. Be personable and friendly!

About page

Content for Your Website

Design other pages your website might have:

Product or Services Page

Frequently Asked Questions

Marketing Plan

Use the example given in *Running a Micro Business* to create a marketing plan. List your marketing methods (business cards, fliers, etc) across the top. List who you can reach with each method and set a reasonable goal. Then break down the goal into smaller steps and assign each a due date.

Who can I reach?					
Goal					
Step 1					
Due Date					
Step 2					
Due Date					
Step 3					
Due Date					

Chapter Ten
Customer Service

In *Running a Micro Business* Chapter Three, I include a long list of customer service ideas. To help you remember them all, use the book to fill in the blanks.

1. _____!

2. Shake _____.

3. Look them _____

4. Say _____ and _____

5. Be _____

6. Leave the place _____

7. Give them _____

8. Give away _____

9. _____ and give a refund

10. Be _____

11. Dress _____

12. Be _____, but keep _____

13. Give customers several ways to _____

14. Leave something they _____

15. Remember _____

16. Listen to complaints and _____

17. Make doing business _____

18. Never, ever _____

19. Return _____ promptly.

20. Pleasantly _____

21. _____ your mistakes.

22. Do not make them _____

23. _____ them.

24. Do a little _____

25. Give _____

26. Ask, "_____?"

27. Ask, "Do you have _____?"

Answers: 1. Smile, 2. hands, 3. in the eye, 4. please, thank you, 5. on time, 6. cleaner than you found it, 7. more than they expected, 8. giving something for free, 9. Apologize, 10. flexible, 11. can pass along, 12. nicely, 13. friendly, a level of professionalism, 14. contact you, 15. your customer's name, 16. do not make excuses, 17. easy for your customer, 18. argue, 19. phone calls and emails, 20. surprise, 21. Admit, 22. wait, 23. Acknowledge, 24. extra, 25. options, 26. What else can I do for you, 27. any friends or neighbors who could use me/my product.

Chapter Eleven
Record Keeping

Classifying Business or Personal Expenses

In *Running a Micro Business* Chapter Four on Record Keeping, micro business owners are encouraged to keep personal and business expenses separate. One way to do this is to mark each transaction in a checkbook as either personal or business. Mark each of the following transactions as B for business or S for self. Some transactions may be for either business or for self; Mark these E for Either. The answers are on the following page. Discuss your answers with your class, group or a business mentor

1. Gas receipt

2. Office supplies

3. Domain name for website

4. Internet service provider monthly bill

5. Restaurant receipt

6. Post Office receipt

7. Target receipt

8. Paypal for a purchase of software

9. Designs by Joe for an ad design

10. Email service monthly fee

A File Folder System for Record Keeping

In *Running a Micro Business*, I describe a filing system for classifying business documents. The following documents belong to a craft business. Match the document or receipts with its file folder.

Document

____ 1. Bank statements

____ 2. Receipt from craft store for supplies

____ 3. Sales receipts

____ 4. Reminder to pay parents for internet

____ 5. Copy of invoice sent to Mrs. Jones

____ 6. Receipt from Target for paint

____ 7. Statement from Paypal on sales

____ 8. Bill for booth rental at craft show

____ 9. Deposit slip from bank

File folder

a. Income

b. Checking Account

c. Expenses

d. Accounts Receivable (Who owes you?)

e. Accounts Payable (Who do you owe?)

Answer key:
Clarifying business (B) or personal expenses (S): 1. S, 2. B, 3. B, 4.B, 5. either S or B, 6. either S or B, 7. either S or B, 8. B, 9. B, 10. B

Matching document to file folder: 1. b, 2.c, 3. a, 4. e, 5. d, 6. c, 7. a, 8. c, 9. b

Start Up and Capital Expenses

Tom starts a lawn care business on May 1st, when he gets paid for his first lawn mowing job. Label each transaction as a start up expense, a capital expense or an ordinary business expense (after the business has started). Refer to *Running a Micro Business*, Chapter Four Record Keeping for definitions of start up and capital expenses.

_____ 1. Buy a book for $10 on starting a lawn care business on March 31

_____ 2. Buy a used lawnmower for $60 on April 20

_____ 3. Print fliers for $10 on April 22

_____ 4. Spend $16 on April 25 for gas and oil for the lawnmower

_____ 5. Buy a new blade for mower on May 6 for $24

_____ 6. Spend $36 for gloves and a rake on June 10.

Add up Tom's Start Up expenses

Start Up expenses	Date	Amount
		Word
		word
		word
		words
	Total	Sentence

Add up Tom's Capital Expenses

Capital expenses	Date	Amount	Percent Business Use

Answer key: 1. Start up, 2.Capital, 3. Start up, 4. Start up, 5. Ordinary, 6. Ordinary. Total Start up expenses (book, fliers, gas & oil) is $36. Total capital expense (mower) $60.

Chapter Twelve
Bookkeeping and Software

This chapter will be a practice example of bookkeeping for a teenage micro business. From the facts and data provided, fill in the Income and Expense ledgers and spreadsheets.

Refer to the examples in *Running a Micro Business* Chapter Five. They can guide you on choosing categories of expenses and how to fill in the ledgers. The answers are provided at the end of this chapter. Try to do the problem yourself first, but check your answers after each section so mistakes are not carried forward.

I highly recommend that you do the problem in pencil, so you can correct any errors you might have made. What you label a transaction is not as important as recording the correct amount. For example, you might record "Income: Dance lessons" but someone else might write "Dance lessons on Tuesday." Either label is acceptable if the amount recorded is correct.

Facts and Data for Bookkeeping Practice Problem:

Amanda runs a micro business giving dance lessons to children in her basement. She charges $50 per student for 6 weeks of lessons. Amanda does not offer a refund for missed days or reduce her fee for students that join late, but she does offer a make-up class after the 6-week session ends.

At the start of her 6-week class, Amanda collects $50 from each student. She also sells T-shirts with her tag line "Dance Lessons by Amanda" for $10 each. Amanda pays sales tax of 5% on every T-shirt she sells.

Amanda has a financial goal of buying a used car and she already has $500 in her savings account.

Amanda's expenses are minimal. She had start up expenses of $75 to buy a mirror, a ballet barre and a rug. She purchases water bottles for her students about once a month. Amanda asks her mother to buy water bottles at the grocery and she reimburses her mother in cash. Amanda found a video on ballet for $15 and she plays that while the students arrive or wait for their parents. Amanda decided to have some business cards printed and that is her only advertising expense. Other advertising includes email and phone calls and costs Amanda nothing.

From the facts given, list Amanda's sources of income and categories for her expenses. There is some extra, unneeded information. Can you spot it?

Sources of Income	Categories of Expense

(check your answers at the end of the chapter before continuing)

Income

- On Tuesday January 5, Amanda begins a class and collect payment from 5 students. Three students also purchase a T-shirt.
- On Saturday, January 9, Amanda begins another class with 6 students. Two of them buy T-shirts.
- On February 8, another student joins the Tuesday class and pays $50. She also buys a T-shirt.
- Amanda's conducts 5 more weeks of class.
- On Tuesday, February 23, Amanda starts another class with 4 students. Each of the students pays Amanda $50.
- Saturday, February 27, is the start of a new class with 6 students. Amanda also sells one T-shirt.
- Amanda receives a bank statement dated March 30 showing she has earned $10 of interest on her savings.

Record Amanda's income on the Income Ledger. Check your answers before continuing.

Income Ledger

Date	Source	Amount
Total		

Expenses

- Amanda reimburses her mother $10 for water bottles on January 3, February 8, March 1 and March 16.
- Amanda's business cards were purchased on-line for $24.00 on January 3. She paid using her debit card.
- Amanda purchased a ballet video for $15 on January 7 using a debit card.
- Amanda ordered 20 T-shirts for $6.75 each on February 20. She paid with check number 120.
- Amanda calculates her sales tax to be paid as 5% of all the T-shirts income she has made from January to March 31. She mails check number 121 on March 31.

Record Amanda's expenses on the Expense Ledger.

Expense Ledger

Date	Source	Category	Amount
		Total	

Check your answers before continuing.

Try another method of bookkeeping: recording everything in a spreadsheet instead of income and expense ledgers. Use a software program such as Microsoft Excel or Open Office Calculate. I'll get you started with a few lines from Amanda's income and expense ledgers. Fill in the rest and calculate her totals.

Date	Check Number	Description	Income	Advertising	Supplies	Other	Inventory
Jan 3	cash	water			$10.00		
Jan 3	debit	business cards		$24.00			
Jan 5		Tuesday class, 5 students	$250.00				
Total for quarter							

Finally, summarize Amanda's business for the first quarter January though March.

Summary

Month	Income	Advertising	Supplies	Other	Inventory
January					
February					
March					
Total	0	0	0	0	0

According to the rule of thumb given in *Running a Micro Business* (more than $500 profit in a quarter), does Amanda need meet with her accountant to calculate her taxes?

Using Software for Bookkeeping

In Chapter Six of *Running a Micro Business*, I gave you an idea of when you might start using software for your bookkeeping tasks. Any of the methods listed below can work for your micro business, it just depends on the nature of your business. Keep bookkeeping as simple as possible, especially if you are just starting out. Check which method you will use in your micro business.

❏ Paper bookkeeping with income and expense ledgers

❏ Paper bookkeeping with columns for expenses

❏ Spreadsheet on a computer

❏ Personal money management software.

   Which software?_____

❏ Small business accounting software.

   Which software:_____

Why are you using accounting software?

   ❏   Invoice customers

   ❏   Employee payroll

   ❏   Inventory

Answers to bookkeeping problem

Sources of Income

Dance lessons

Sale of T shirts

Interest from saving account

Categories of Expense

Supplies (water)

Advertising (business cards)

Other (video and sales tax)

Inventory (or Cost Of Goods Sold)

Income Ledger

Date	Source	Amount
Jan 5	Tuesday class, 5 students	$250.00
Jan 5	Sell 3 T-shirts	$30.00
Jan 9	Sat class 6 students	$300.00
Jan 9	Sell 2 T-shirts	$20.00
Feb 8	Tuesday class, 1 student	$50.00
Feb 8	Sell 1 T-shirt	$10.00
Feb 23	Tuesday class 4 students	$200.00
Feb 27	Sat class 6 students	$300.00
Feb 27	Sell 1 T-shirt	$10.00
Mar 30	Interest earned	$10.00

Total $1,180.00

Expenses Ledger

Date	Source	Category	Amount
Jan 3	water	Supplies	$10.00
Jan 3	business cards	Advertising	$24.00
Jan 7	video	Other	$15.00
Feb 8	water	Supplies	$10.00
Mar 1	water	Supplies	$10.00
Mar 16	water	Supplies	$10.00
Mar 31	sales tax	Other	$3.50

The extra, unneeded information was Amanda's start up expenses. She should record her start up expenses and tell her tax preparer about them, as discussed in the chapter on record-keeping, but they are not recorded in her expenses ledger.

Notice that Amanda's purchase of the T-shirts is not recorded in the expenses ledger. Recall in the chapter on record keeping that inventory is not considered an expense. It should be recorded and shared with Amanda's tax preparer, but not recorded in her expenses ledger.

Date	Check Number	Description	Income	Advertising	Supplies	Other	Inventory
Jan 3	cash	water			$10.00		
Jan 3	debit	business cards		$24.00			
Jan 5		Tuesday class, 5 students	$250.00				
Jan 5		Sell 3 T-shirts	$30.00				
Jan 7	debit	video				$15.00	
Jan 9		Sat class 6 students	$300.00				
Jan 9		Sell 2 T-shirts	$20.00				
Feb 8		Tuesday class, 1 student	$50.00				
Feb 8		Sell 1 T-shirt	$10.00				
Feb 8	cash	water			$10.00		
Feb 20	120	Buy 20 T-shirts					$135.00
Feb 23		Tuesday class 4 students	$200.00				
Feb 27		Sat class 6 students	$300.00				
Feb 27		Sell 1 T-shirt	$10.00				
Mar 1	cash	water			$10.00		
Mar 16	cash	water			$10.00		
Mar 30		Interest earned	$10.00				
Mar 31	121	sales tax				$3.50	
		Total for quarter	$1,180.00	$24.00	$40.00	$18.50	$135.00

Summary					
Month	**Income**	**Advertising**	**Supplies**	**Other**	**Inventory**
January	$660.00	$24.00	$10.00	$15.00	
February	$510.00		$10.00		$135.00
March	$10.00		$20.00	$3.50	
Total	$1,180.00	$24.00	$40.00	$18.50	$135.00

Yes, Amanda should meet with an accountant. Her profit for the quarter is $963 (including all her expenses and the purchase of T-shirts) which is more than my rule of thumb of $500 profit in a quarter.

$1180— $24—$40—$18.50—$135 = $962.50

Amanda's accountant explained that if she continued making similar income in the rest of the year that she will probably not owe any federal income tax, but she will owe another type of tax called Self Employment tax. Self Employment tax is the same as Social Security and Medicare taxes for self employed business owners. Her accountant calculates her Self Employment taxes will be approximately $540 for the full year, if she continues to make a profit as she did from January to March. The accountant encourages Amanda to set aside some of her profit to pay for these taxes at the end of the year. Following her accountant's advice, Amanda sets aside $135 for taxes for this quarter (about 15% of her profit).

Money and Taxes in a Micro Business covers taxes in more detail.

Chapter Thirteen
Names, Numbers and Insurance

In *Running a Micro Business* Chapter Seven, you read that sometimes a micro does not need a business name.

Business Names

Will you use your personal name or create a business name?

Business Name: _____

Visit **www.business.gov/register/business-name/dba.html** and research your local or state requirements for registering a business name.

Registering a business name in my city or state:

Licenses

Research your local business regulations concerning:

- Vendor licenses if you will sell a product and collect sales tax

- Health permits if you sell food items

- Zoning rules if you plan to work from home

Your research can begin online at **www.business.gov/register/licenses-and-permits/**. Or try a Google search on your city name and "business license." Additionally, you may need to call your local government office and ask about businesses licenses, vendor licenses, health regulations and zoning permits.

Business licenses or permits required in my city or state:

Sole Proprietorship

In Chapter Seven of *Running a Micro Business,* I recommended that a teenage-owned micro business be formed as a sole proprietorship for several reasons. Fill in the blanks using the book.

1. Quick and _____.

2. No _____ agreements.

3. No _____ status.

4. Sole proprietorships are easy to _____.

5. Sole proprietorships are easy to _____.

6. _____ tax structure.

7. No _____ needed.

8. You keep _____

9. No _____ to keep happy.

Numbers

For your micro business tax forms, will you use

❏ Your Social Security Number (SSN) or

❏ An Employer Identification Number (EIN). Why?_____

Answers: 1. easy to start, 2. partnership, 3. corporate, 4. close, 5. understand, 6.Simplest, 7. lawyer, 8. your profits, 9. investors

Insurance

In Chapter Eight of *Running a Micro Business*, there are several types of insurance listed. Discuss what insurance you might need for your micro business with your parents and a business mentor. Fill in the following for your micro business:

Type of Insurance	Reason for Needing It	Agent Name	Phone	Price Quote

Could your business be added as a rider to your parents' homeowner's policy? Call your parents' insurance agent and ask for a quote.

Agent Name & Number	Insurance Coverage	Cost

Limited Liability Company

Does your micro business have any of the risks mentioned in the book?

❏ Personal service   ❏ Childcare

❏ Advice or consulting   ❏ Potential injury

❏ Food preparation   ❏ Employees

After reading about the pros and cons of LLC status, will you apply for LLC status for your micro business?

Research the cost to form a Limited Liability Company in your state. Start with a Google search for your state's Secretary of State website. Then search the site for the application for Limited Liability Company. Read through the application paperwork, paying attention to the requirements such as names and dates. Look for additional requirements after the initial application.

Cost: $_____

Initial Filing Requirements: _____

_____

Additional filing requirements and fees: _____

_____

Questions you have about forming an LLC to ask a business mentor or lawyer.

Chapter Fourteen
Time Management

In *Running a Micro Business*, I mention that goals should be SMART:

Specific

Measurable

Action Oriented

Reasonable

Timely

List of few goals you have for your micro business. They may be financial goals, or something you wish to learn.

Goals:

Fill in the chart with your business goals paying attention to the SMART guidelines

Goal (SM)	Action Steps (A)	Obstacles(R)	Finish Date (T)	Who Can Help

To Do Lists

A To Do list can come in many varieties. Here are a few samples. Use several until you find one that you prefer to organize all your tasks.

Due Today

Due This Week

Due This Month

Task	Priority

High Priority

	Completed
1	
2	
3	

Medium Priority

1	
2	
3	

Low Priority

1	
2	
3	

Sample To Do Lists

This sample To Do list uses a calendar page to list different tasks to be done each day.

Monday	Tuesday	Wednesday	Thursday	Friday	Saturday

Time Survey:

Chart how you currently spend your time. Fill in as you go about your week.

Daily Schedule

Time	Monday	Tuesday	Wednesday	Thursday	Friday	Saturday	Sunday
6:00 AM							
7:00 AM							
8:00 AM							
9:00 AM							
10:00 AM							
11:00 AM							
12:00 PM							
1:00 PM							
2:00 PM							
3:00 PM							
4:00 PM							
5:00 PM							
6:00 PM							
7:00 PM							
8:00 PM							
9:00 PM							
10:00 PM							
11:00 PM							
12:00 AM							

Schedule

Chart how you *want* to spend your time.

Daily Schedule

Time	Monday	Tuesday	Wednesday	Thursday	Friday	Saturday	Sunday
6:00 AM							
7:00 AM							
8:00 AM							
9:00 AM							
10:00 AM							
11:00 AM							
12:00 PM							
1:00 PM							
2:00 PM							
3:00 PM							
4:00 PM							
5:00 PM							
6:00 PM							
7:00 PM							
8:00 PM							
9:00 PM							
10:00 PM							
11:00 PM							
12:00 AM							

Conclusion

I hope this workbook has helped you launch and run a micro business. If you have made it to the end, you have accomplished a lot! Look back over how far you have come. You have reason to be proud of your efforts.

I hope this is not the end of the entrepreneurial life for you. You have so much knowledge to apply to future business. Where will the future take you? We do not know, but perhaps you will start another business someday. It might be another micro business or something larger. The sky is the limit!

I encourage you to keep on learning. There is more to learn every day about running a business. Be sure to visit my website **MicroBusinessForTeens.com** where I will be constantly uploading new information, offering classes and videos.

About the Author

Carol Topp, CPA, owner of **www.CarolToppCPA.com** and **MicroBusinessFor-Teens.com** helps people, especially teenagers, start their own small businesses.

Carol was born and raised in Racine, Wisconsin and graduated from Purdue University with a degree in engineering. She worked ten years for the US Navy as a cost analyst before staying home with her two daughters. While being a stay-at-home mom, Carol took accounting classes via distance learning. In 2000, Carol received her CPA license and opened her own practice.

She is a member of the Ohio Society of CPAs, the National Association of Tax Professionals and the Society of Nonprofit Organizations. Carol has presented numerous workshops on money management, business start up, taxes, budgeting and homeschooling to various community, church and homeschool groups.

She has authored several books including:
- *Homeschool Co-ops: How to Start Them, Run Them and Not Burn Out*
- *Information in a Nutshell: Business Tips and Taxes for Writers*
- *Teens and Taxes: A Guide for Parents and Teenagers*

Carol lives in Cincinnati, Ohio with her husband and two daughters where she runs her micro business from her home.

The **Micro Business for Teens** series has these titles.

Starting a Micro Business covers getting an idea, making a business plan, starting without debt and doing research.

Running a Micro Business covers record keeping, inventory, selling products, time management, marketing and customer service.

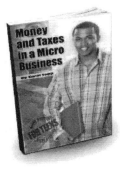

Money and Taxes covers financial statements, income taxes, tax deductions, sales tax, employees and working with an accountant.

The **Micro Business for Teens Workbook** is designed for individual or group study. Put into practice what you read in *Starting a Micro Business* and *Running a Micro Business*.

Also available are audios, virtual classes, webinars, and video instruction on starting and running a micro business.

Available at **MicroBusinessForTeens.com**